OSPREY MILITARY

MEN-AT-ARMS SERIES 292

KING GEORGE'S ARMY
1740-1793:(3)

Text by
STUART REID
Colour plates by
MIKE CHAPPELL

First published in Great Britain in 1996 by
Osprey, an imprint of Reed Consumer Books Ltd.
Michelin House, 81 Fulham Road,
London SW3 6RB
and Auckland, Melbourne, Singapore and Toronto

ISBN 1 85532 565 9

Filmset in Great Britain by KDI, Newton le Willows
Printed through World Print Ltd, Hong Kong

Publisher's Note

Readers may wish to study this title in conjunction with the
following Osprey publications:

MAA 285   *King George's Army (1)*
MAA 289   *King George's Army (2)*
MAA 39   *British Army in North America*
MAA 118   *The Jacobite Rebellions*
MAA 261   *18th Century Highlanders*

Artist's note

Readers may care to note that the original paintings from
which the colour plates in this book were prepared are
available for private sale. All reproduction copyright what-
soever is retained by the publisher. All enquiries should be
addressed to:

Paul Chappell
c/o 14 Downlands
Walmer
Deal
Kent CT14 7XA

The publishers regret that they can enter into no corre-
spondence upon this matter.

Volumes 1 and 2 of *King George's Army* covered both regular
and auxiliary infantry units (see MAA 285 and 289). This
present volume deals with cavalry units of all descriptions
and those troops administered by the Board of Ordnance –
the artillery, engineers and artificers.

INTRODUCTION

In 1740, there were some 500 cavalry officers on the regular establishment, compared to about 1,450 infantry officers. The inevitable expansion of the army during the War of the Austrian Succession saw the number of infantry (and marine) officers increase to about 2,500, but the number of cavalry officers remained constant. Indeed, only two new regiments were raised during the war, both of them at the height of the Jacobite emergency in 1745. After 1748, the number of cavalry officers again dropped to around 450 against some 1,650 infantry officers.

The outbreak of the Seven Years War again slightly lifted the cavalry total this time to 600. But, by contrast, nearly 4,000 infantry officers were carried on the Army List at the height of the conflict. Further fluctuations followed the end of the war in 1763 and the American War of Independence 1775-1783, but although the total number of cavalrymen had remained higher than in 1740, their relative importance was less. In 1740 cavalrymen accounted for a quarter of the King's officers (excluding Ordnance officers), but by 1793 that proportion had dropped to only a sixth.

However, the figures can be slightly misleading. The steady expansion of the infantry largely reflected the increased need to man imperial garrisons. In operations closer to home though, the perceived importance of the cavalry was undiminished.

During the War of the Austrian Succession two troops of Horse Guards, one troop of Horse Grenadier Guards, the Blues, two other regiments of Horse and seven Dragoon regiments served in Flanders – a total of ten regiments, besides the Horse Guards, while 14 British cavalry regiments served in Germany during the Seven Years War. At the same time 22 infantry regiments had served

Officer's grenadier cap, 2nd (Royal North British) Dragoons. The Greys were famously distinguished not only by their grey horses, but also by the wearing of grenadier caps in place of hats. The prominent display of the garter star rather than the star of St. Andrew is rather surprising but also appears in the depiction of a trooper of the Greys in the 1742 Cloathing Book. *The replacement of the usual white horse on the little flap is also unusual, but a distinction shared at this time with the 21st Foot. (Author)*

in Flanders and 17 in Germany. By contrast, during the American War of Independence, only two regular cavalry regiments; the 16th and 17th Dragoons saw service, although they were of course supported by a number of locally raised provincial units.

The British Army had three classes of cavalry in 1740: Household units, Horse and Dragoons.

Trooper 13th Dragoons as depicted in the 1742 Cloathing Book. *This uniform survived virtually unchanged in the 1751 Warrant, but the elaborately decorated saddle housings and holster caps were replaced by a much simpler style sometime before Morier painted a trooper in 1748. (Trustees of the National Museums of Scotland)*

Highest in order of precedence, the Household cavalry comprised four grossly over-officered troops of red-coated Horse Guards (amalgamated into two troops in 1746) and two troops of Horse Grenadiers. Although unquestionably a social elite, the fact that the Horse Guards rarely ventured outside London did nothing for their military efficiency. Only the Horse Grenadiers, originally raised as specialist Dragoons were reckoned to have any real military value and in 1788 both they and the two remaining troops of Horse Guards were amalgamated to form the Lifeguards.

After the Household cavalry proper came the Royal Regiment of Horse Guards (the 'Blues'),

and seven other regiments of Horse. The greater part of the British Army's cavalry however comprised 14 regiments of Dragoons – increased to 15 in 1746. These had originally been no more than mounted infantry and were still looked down upon as such by the Horse. But although regularly trained as infantrymen in the platoon exercise, in reality there was very little – other than their uniforms and rates of pay – to distinguish them from the Horse.

In 1746, the same economy drive which saw the four troops of Horse Guards reduced to two, also saw a change in status for three of the regiments of Horse. Mindful of the fact that the differences between Horse and Dragoons were very largely cosmetic ones, it was decided to convert the regiments of Horse into Dragoons. However, in order to preserve the all important order of precedence and to sweeten the pill a little, those converted regiments were called Dragoon Guards. The Blues, who had previously ranked as the 1st Horse, were spared. Otherwise, there ought, in theory to have been seven regiments of Dragoon Guards and 15 of Dragoons. But in fact, Dublin Castle for reasons best known to itself decided against converting the four regiments of Horse then maintained on the separate Irish Establishment.

As a result, the 2nd or King's Horse became the 1st or King's Dragoon Guards, the 3rd or Queen's Horse became the 2nd Dragoon Guards and the 4th became the 3rd Dragoon Guards. The 5th to 8th Horse were then redesignated as the 1st to 4th (Irish) Horse, although eventually they too finally became Dragoon Guards in 1789.

This round of alterations did not affect the total number of units, and consequently the disbandment of the short-lived 15th Dragoons in 1748 left the army with the same number of line cavalry regiments as in 1740, except that they now comprised three regiments of Dragoon Guards, four regiments of Horse and 14 regiments of Dragoons. Each category was distinguished one from another only by various peculiarities of dress.

Co-operation with the Imperial army in Flanders during the 1740s had pointed up the usefulness of light cavalry and the 15th Dragoons,

Guidon, 4th Dragoons (?) 1740s. Only one guidon was carried by each squadron of which the first, or King's, was to be of crimson damask and the others in the regimental facing colour. Only two Dragoon regiments had green facings at this time – the 4th and the 13th. Since the fringing is silver it may be inferred that this guidon was carried by the former regiment as Gardiner's 13th had gold lace. Unauthorised badges, such as this stag and motto **Rouze**, *were supposedly suppressed in about 1743 but in practice only seem to have been replaced as they wore out – or were lost. In 1746 the 13th lost a 'curious fine' guidon at Falkirk bearing the motto* **Britons Strike Home**. *(Author)*

originally raised during the Jacobite emergency as Kingston's 10th Horse, are said to have been trained as hussars. General Henry Hawley (who was nobody's fool despite his quite undeserved reputation as a vicious martinet) had in fact advocated the raising of such a unit as early as 1728. But to Cumberland's dismay the regiment, although a good one, was disbanded in 1748. It was all the more galling of course that the 13th and 14th Dragoons, who had distinguished themselves during the late Jacobite emergency only by the speed with which they ran away every time they met the enemy, were retained on the Irish Establishment.

The outbreak of the Seven Years War in 1756 brought a slight increase in the size of the cavalry. At first, as was the case with the infantry, this simply took the form of an augmentation in the strength of existing units carried on the English Establishment. But because of the desperate need for some kind of light cavalry 11 additional troops authorised on 14 April 1757, were intended to fill that role. After that, there was no looking back and beginning in March 1759 Letters of Service were granted for no less than seven new cavalry regiments, all of them designated as Light Dragoons. Similarly all the new cavalry units raised during the American War of Independence

and those raised after 1793 were also designated as Light Dragoons. The 19th, 20th and 21st Light Dragoons were actually formed by brigading together the newly raised Light Troops of the Heavy cavalry regiments and by 1783 nearly all the old regiments of 'heavy' dragoons had been converted to light cavalry.

Unfortunately, although attended by considerable enthusiasm this preoccupation with the merits of light cavalry in reality extended little further than the intricacies of military millinery. The sad fact of the matter was that, in contrast to the solid professionalism of the British infantry, all too many cavalry officers did indeed subscribe to the not entirely apocryphal view that their chief function was to lend some tone to what might otherwise be a vulgar brawl. And their tactical

Cornet, 8th Horse. Said to have been carried and defended by Cornet Richardson at Dettingen in 1743, this rather fine cornet is of crimson damask with a gold fringe and the arms of General Ligonier. The small union in the canton appears to have been suppressed in 1743. (Author)

repertoire was almost entirely limited to the charge.

In 1758 the intention had been very different. The *Weekly Journal* for 23 May reported approvingly on the Light Troop of the 11th Dragoons, then preparing to take part in one of the raids on the French coast: 'The hussars of the nine regiments are now preparing to go on the expedition. The flower of these Hussars is the Troop commanded by Captain Lindsay quartered at Maidenhead where they have been practising the Prussian exercise and for some days have been digging trenches and leaping over them, also leaping high hedges with broad ditches on the other side. Their Captain on Saturday last swam with his horse over the Thames and back again and the whole Troop were yesterday to swim the river.'

This was all well and good, but the work done by the likes of William Lindsay was undone when the first of the new Light Dragoon regiments went into action. In July 1760, the newly landed 15th Light Dragoons were ordered to take part in a heavy raid on the French garrison of Marburg. En route the raiders unexpectedly ran into five French battalions near Emsdorf. An attempt to surprise this detachment failed, but after the 15th cut the Marburg road the French tried to escape across country. One battalion got clean away but the others were twice charged by the 15th. Finally, as the exhausted dragoons formed for a third charge the French – actually a German regiment, the Royal Baverie – decided that they had had enough and surrendered.

In the euphoria which followed this notable feat of arms, the fact that they had lost 125 men and 168 horses in the action and afterwards had to be sent back to Hanover to reorganise was quietly overlooked. Thereafter, the mundane demands of outpost work and skirmishing were subordinated to training for the charge and in the hope of another such glorious enterprise as Emsdorf. The regiment made so much of this victory that they emblazoned the details on their helmet plates

There was little chance of finding a similar triumph during the American War of Independence. While the infantry learned valuable lessons there, the cavalry learned little. Much of the work done there did indeed centre around the demanding skills of outpost work, reconnaissance and skirmishing. But only two regular dragoon regiments, the 16th and 17th, served there. Even the 16th came home in 1778 and their influence at home was negligible.

Consequently, at the outset of the great war with Revolutionary France in 1793, there was virtually nothing save their uniforms to distinguish Light Dragoons from their heavier brethren. This point was dramatically emphasised by the action at Villers-en-Cauchies on 24 April 1794, which again involved the 15th Light Dragoons. Two squadrons of the regiment, together with two squadrons of the Austrian Leopold Hussars, charged and dispersed six battalions of French infantry. From then on, it was useless to expect British light cavalry to do anything more complicated than to charge straight at the enemy.

ORGANISATION

In 1740, each troop of Horse Guards mustered no fewer than 18 officers, comprising a colonel, first and second lieutenant colonels, first and second majors, four 'exempts', four brigadiers, four sub-brigadiers and an adjutant. When the four troops were being consolidated into two at the end of 1746, they were ordered to be completed to 150 privates apiece.

The line regiments however, including the Blues, were much more conventionally officered, and were normally made up of six or occasionally seven troops, each commanded by a captain, lieutenant and a cornet. The latter was the equivalent of the infantry ensign. As in the infantry three of the troop commanders were also field officers: the colonel, lieutenant colonel and major, and the colonel's own troop was actually led by a captain-lieutenant.

In addition to its officers, each troop of Dragoons or Dragoon Guards comprised three sergeants, three corporals, two drummers, and 59 troopers. The establishment also included a hautbois or oboist in each troop, but this individual existed only on paper, his pay being one of the colonel's traditional perquisites.

In action, cavalry troops were normally paired

Colonel James Gardiner, 13th Dragoons (1688-1745). Born in Linlithgow, the son of another professional soldier, Gardiner was killed at Prestonpans in 1745 while commanding the 13th Dragoons. (NMS)

off to form squadrons and drew up three men deep, either in line or with two squadrons up and the third in reserve. It was possible to vary this practice if the tactical situation demanded it. At Prestonpans in 1745, General Cope formed both his Dragoon regiments in two ranks deep rather than the usual three. In the following year at Culloden, General Hawley deployed the two regular Dragoon regiments in their individual troops rather than pairing them off into squadrons. In both cases this was done because the likelihood of action against hostile cavalry was nonexistent.

Although trained for dismounted action, British cavalrymen almost invariably went into action sitting on their horses' backs. The night battle at Clifton in 1745 appears to be the only occasion

Colonel Gardiner of the 13th Dragoons lived at Bankton House on the fringe of the Prestonpans battlefield. Breaches were made in the park walls in the hours before the battle in order to allow free passage through them by General Cope's troops. The subsequent repairs to the wall linking the main house with one of two flanking pavilions can clearly be seen. (Author)

during the period in which extensive use was made of dismounted dragoons.

UNIFORMS AND EQUIPMENT

As in the infantry the clothing and equipment issued to each soldier was set out in the *Regulations for the Cloathing of His Majesty's Forces in Time of Peace 20 Nov. 1729.* This specified:

For a trooper
A new cloth coat, well lined with serge.
A new waistcoat.
A new laced hat.
A pair of new large buff gloves, with stiff tops, once in two years.

A pair of new boots, as they shall be found wanting.

As it is difficult to fix a period of time for providing saddles, it is to be left to the judgement of the general officer, who may be appointed to review them.
Housings, (holster) caps, new horse furniture, bitts, and stirrup-irons; cloaks faced with the livery of the regiment, entirely new; and new buff or buff coloured cross-belts, to be provided as they shall be wanting.
The second mounting is to consist of new-laced hats, and horse collars.

For a dragoon
A new cloth coat, well lined with serge.
A new waistcoat.
A pair of new breeches.
A new laced hat.
A pair of new large buff-coloured gloves with stiff tops.
A pair of new boots, as they shall be wanting.
Saddles to be left to the judgement of the general officer who may be appointed to review them.
Housings, [holster] caps, new horse furniture, bitts and stirrup-irons; and cloaks faced with the

livery of the regiment, entirely new, as they shall be wanting.

New buff or buff-coloured accoutrements; viz. A shoulder-belt, with a pouch, a waist-belt, sufficient to carry the sword, with a place to receive the bayonet and sling for the arms, such as the general officers, appointed to inspect the cloathing, shall approve of, as they shall be wanting.

The second mounting is to consist of new-laced hats, gloves, and horse-collars.

Perhaps the most striking difference between these lists and the similar ones relating to the provision of clothing for infantrymen is the degree to which the clothing and equipment issued was expected to last longer. Instead of a regular two year replacement cycle the cavalryman could expect to be clothed every year – including a new waistcoat and not a red one cut down from the previous year's coat, but everything else was to be replaced only as and when required.

An inspection report on the 4th 'Irish' Horse in 1771 disapprovingly noted that the boots had been received as long ago as 1767. Consequently, while the commanders of infantry regiments were required to certify annually that they had supplied their men with the clothing to which they were entitled, commanders of cavalry units only had to do so every two years.

Regiments of Horse, Dragoon Guards, Dragoons and Light Dragoons were distinguished in the following ways. Regiments of Horse had fairly narrow lapels which stretched from the collar to the hem of the coat. Dragoon Guards had smaller, broader, 'half lapels' like those worn by infantrymen. Dragoons had no lapels at all, but Light Dragoons wore narrow lapels similar to those worn by infantrymen after 1768. The 16th were, at first, an exception and Morier's painting

Contemporary map of the battle of Falkirk (17 January 1746). General Hawley's three regiments of Dragoons were posted on the left of his front line and opened the battle with an unsuccessful attack against the Jacobite infantry. A miserable performance was then compounded by riding over the loyalist Glasgow Volunteers in their flight – and naturally being shot up by them in the process. (NMS)

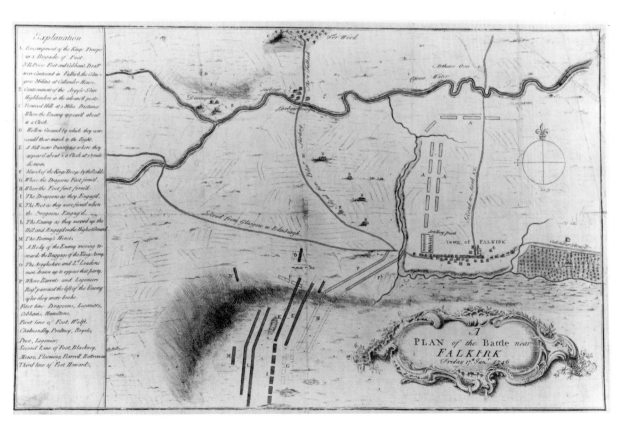

Drummer's cap, 13th Dragoons. Like those worn by infantry drummers this cap has a rather lower front than a grenadier cap and the bag or stocking therefore hangs down at the back. The trophies displayed on the front are simply a conventional design and do not reflect any particular battle honours – indeed the only active service seen by the 13th Dragoons throughout the 18th century consisted of running away from the rebels at Prestonpans and Falkirk. (Author)

shows the original uniform to have been a single breasted coat of 'heavy' dragoon style with black collar and cuffs. They did however subsequently adopt lapels.

Apart from their leather, copper or brass helmets, the Light Troops attached to regiments of Dragoon Guards and Dragoons during the Seven Years War wore the uniform of their parent regiment – that is, with half lapels for Dragoon Guards and no lapels for Dragoons. With the exception of the Blues, all cavalry regiments wore red coats until 1784 when blue jackets were adopted by Light Dragoons. At that point, those regiments which had previously worn blue facings were ordered to adopt red ones instead.

Under King George II, cavalry regiments were also distinguished from their infantry counterparts by generally wearing waistcoats and breeches of the facing colour rather than plain red ones. In 1768, however, they too were ordered to adopt white linings and small-clothes, although inspection reports reveal that a number of units wore buff linings in the early 1770s.

The trumpeters and kettledrummers of the Horse (and Dragoon Guards) and drummers of Dragoon regiments wore the traditional reversed coat colours liberally decorated with lace. Dragoon drummers had the same small mitre style caps worn by infantry drummers prior to 1768, but trumpeters of Horse and Dragoon Guards wore the same cocked hats as the troopers and officers. Light Dragoon drums and trumpets however wore helmets from the outset. This distinctive clothing reflected the fact that drums and trumpets were signallers rather than musicians and had to be readily identified by officers in the midst of battle. Consequently many regiments also went so far as to mount them on greys as a further distinction, although inspection reports reveal that this was far from being a universal practice.

Cavalrymen required more necessaries than their infantry counterparts and these included black woollen gaiters for dismounted drills and guards, half gaiters, forage caps, curry combs etc. and 'frocks'. These were presumably some kind of smocks to be worn for stable duties – although a 1759 order to the Greys laid down that they were to be worn over coats on the march, perhaps because the roads they were travelling on were particularly dusty at the time.

Accoutrements comprised a sword belt, worn over the right shoulder by Horse and around the waist by the Horse Grenadier Guards, Dragoons and Dragoon Guards, and either a carbine belt or a cartridge box and sling, according to arm. Camp Equipage issued by the Board of Ordnance included the usual canteens and haversacks, and picket poles. On the march these were strapped to the trooper's firelock and if time permitted were thrown away at the commencement of an action.

Weapons were somewhat more varied. Generally speaking at the outset of the period all cavalrymen carried broadswords (or occasionally single-edged backswords) with basket hilts. These hilts were often Scottish in origin, differing from those carried by highlanders by an oval ring set into the inside of the basket to allow the trooper to hold sword and reins simultaneously. As the swords were purchased by the colonel there was no fixed pattern and particularly after the introduction of Light Dragoons a number of varieties abounded. Not until 1788 was there any real attempt at standardisation.

Most cavalrymen also carried a pair of pistols, though Light Dragoons were originally supposed to have only one. In theory Dragoons were supposed to thrust their pistols into their belts when dismounted but there is no indication that they did so at Clifton in 1745.

All cavalrymen also carried a carbine of some description. Again there were a number of patterns in use. Until 1770, Dragoons carried a .65 Short Land Pattern firelock with a 42-inch barrel and a wooden ramrod. They were also equipped with a bayonet for it. On march past in review order they were expected to carry their firelocks with bayonets fixed. Doubtless to their dismay, Dragoons Guards were also encumbered with this weapon after their conversion in 1746.

The regiments of Horse were equipped instead with a slightly lighter carbine which, after 1757 at least, had a barrel length of 37 inches and was of .65 or .68 calibre. It was fully stocked to the muzzle and, in place of the usual sling fitted to Dragoon firelocks, it had a ring and bar fitted over the sideplate. This arrangement permitted it, in theory, to be clipped to the carbine belt so that it could be fired from horseback, though it is questionable whether this was ever done. Normally the carbine was strapped to the saddle, butt downwards in Dragoon style.

Light Dragoons on the other hand were in theory expected to skirmish on horseback using their carbines. Kingston's 10th Horse were certainly described as doing so, although it was not until they were taken over by the Duke of Cumberland as the 15th Dragoons that they received a special carbine. This was of .65 calibre with a 42-inch barrel capable of taking a bayonet. Fitted with both an infantry sling and a ring and rather large bar for attaching to a carbine belt, it only really differed from the Short Land Pattern normally carried by Dragoons in its lighter calibre. Having seen comparatively little use these

weapons were appropriated by the Horse Grenadier Guards when the 15th were disbanded in 1748. Subsequently this weapon formed the pattern for the Heavy Dragoon Carbine of 1770.

The Light Dragoon Carbine of 1756 was rather handier with a 36-inch barrel but, in 1760, General Elliot of the 15th Dragoons designed a still shorter one with a 28-inch barrel. Although generally agreed to be an improvement this

Artillery officer 1742, after a contemporary watercolour sketch. The chief points of interest are the comparatively plain appearance of the uniform and his being armed with a fusil. His waistcoat and breeches are scarlet in contrast to the blue small-clothes worn by gunners. (Author)

important, if seldom used, facility to fix a bayonet on to it. In the 1780s experiments were also made with rifled carbines.

Each cavalryman was also provided with harness and saddle housings for his horse. In 1742 the latter, comprising a shabraque or decorative blanket and a pair of holster caps (covers), were quite elaborate with what appears to have been an embroidered edging enlivened by knights' helmets and trophies of arms. By 1748, however, they had been replaced by a much simpler pattern. Probably introduced at the Duke of Cumberland's behest, they displayed the regiment's facing colour and were edged with coloured stripes. The shabraque bore a cartouche with the regiment's number surrounded by a Union wreath, while the holster caps had the Royal cypher in the middle and the number was repeated on the edging – for example, XIII D for 13th Dragoons.

Gunner, Royal Artillery, 1742, after a contemporary watercolour sketch. The coat at this period is substantially unlaced but by 1748 when David Morier painted the train at Roermond in Holland a considerable amount of yellow tape binding had appeared. Although depicted here as carrying only a linstock, large powder-horn and brass-hilted hanger, Morier's painting shows that firelocks were also carried on active service. (Author)

REGIMENTAL DISTINCTIONS

The details here are all taken from the 1742 *Cloathing Book*, Morier's paintings c1748, and the Clothing Warrants of 1751 and 1768. Under the 1768 Warrant, coloured waistcoats and breeches were replaced by white ones and coat linings became either buff or white. Other variations are culled from the inspection reports of various dates and officers' portraits. With the exception of the 1st Horse (Blues), all regiments wore red coats until the 1784 when blue jackets were adopted by light Dragoons.

1st Horse (Royal Regiment of Horseguards)
Blue coats, red facings & waistcoat, blue breeches. No lace on coat. Buff small-clothes worn after 1768.

1st (King's) Dragoon Guards
Blue facings, waistcoat and breeches. Buff small clothes 1768. Yellow lace with buttons arranged in pairs. Red furniture, latterly with "Royal" lace: yellow with a blue stripe. Drummers mounted on greys.

weapon was fully stocked to the muzzle, pre-cluding the use of a bayonet. In 1773 though Elliot produced a second version again with a 28-inch barrel, which this time could be fitted with a bayonet. This version was adopted as the standard Light Dragoon carbine. Another Light Dragoon carbine, issued to the 21st (Royal Forresters) was very similar to the first pattern Elliot except for a better standard of workmanship and the all

Lieutenant Edward Harvey, 10th Dragoons, 1740s.
Harvey (1718-1778) entered the army as a Cornet in the
10th Dragoons in 1741 and remained with that regiment
until gaining a Captaincy in the 7th Dragoons in 1747.
Promoted to Major in 1751 he became Lieutenant Colonel
of the 6th (Inniskilling) Dragoons in 1754 and was
promoted to full Colonel in 1760. A Major General in 1762
he briefly commanded the 12th Dragoons 1763-4 and then

the 3rd (Irish) Horse until 1775 when he resumed
command of the 6th Dragoons. He died in 1778 while
simultaneously holding that post, serving as Adjutant
General, Governor of Portsmouth and sitting as the
Member of Parliament for Harwich. Interestingly although
his coat lining and gorget patches are yellow (the 10th's
facing colour), his rather plain cuffs are red. (Original in
Dundee Art Gallery, photo courtesy of NMS)

Captain Lord Robert Kerr. A Scotsman, he was killed at Culloden while commanding the grenadier company of Barrell's 4th Foot. (NMS)

2nd (Queen's) Dragoon Guards

Buff facings, waistcoat and breeches. Black facings ordered 1783 but not noted until 1785. Yellow lace with buttons set three and three. White small-clothes instead of buff ordered 1774. Red furniture, by 1768 this was buff with 'royal' lace. Bay horses 1768. Drummers and farriers mounted on greys 1776.

3rd (Prince of Wales) Dragoon Guards

White facings and waistcoat, red breeches (white by 1748). Yellow lace with buttons set two and two – a report of 1768 comments on buff tape button loops instead of yellow. White furniture, 'Royal' lace. Trumpeters on greys and farriers on blacks 1776

1st (Irish) Horse – 4th Royal Irish Dragoon Guards 1788

Blue facings, waistcoat and breeches (pale blue by 1748). Officers wearing buff waistcoat and breeches 1768. Dragoon style clothing and accoutrements were not altered to the 'Dragoon' pattern until 1790 although NCOs had 'Dragoon' style uniforms in 1788. Yellow lace – white by 1768 with buttons set two and two. Blue furniture, white lace with red stripe. Trumpeters mounted on greys 1769

2nd (Irish) Horse – 5th Dragoon Guards 1788

Green facings, waistcoat and breeches. 'Full Green' facings 1768, but yellow in 1788. White lace, yellow by 1768 and back to white in 1788 with buttons set two and two.

Green furniture, white lace with red stripe 1768. Yellow furniture, white lace with green stripe ordered in 1788 but old (ie. green) furniture still noted as late as 1792. Trumpeters on bays 1768 and 1775.

3rd (Irish) Horse – 6th Dragoon Guards or Carabineers 1788

Pale yellow facings, buff linings, waistcoat and breeches. White facings by 1769. White lace with buttons set two and two. Buff furniture, then white edged with yellow lace bearing black stripe. Trumpeters on long-tailed greys 1769

4th (Irish) Horse – 7th (Princess Royal's) Dragoon Guards 1788

Black facings, buff small clothes – white 1788. Yellow lace with buttons set two and two. Buff furniture – white 1788 – white lace with black stripe. Trumpeters on greys 1772.

1st (Royal) Dragoons

Blue facings and waistcoat, red breeches (blue by 1748). Yellow lace, buttons set two and two. Sergeants had blue sashes in 1753. Blue furniture, red by 1768 with 'Royal' lace. Drummers and Farriers initially mounted on greys, but blacks by 1777. All horses long-tailed.

2nd (Royal North British) Dragoons

Blue facings, waistcoats and breeches. White lace, buttons set two and two.

Cloth grenadier caps worn by all ranks until 1778, then black bearskin ones. Officers' bearskins 'handsomely' embroidered and ornamented. White accoutrements. Blue furniture with 'Royal' lace. Whole regiment mounted on greys.

Allegedly taken by the French at Fontenoy in 1745 this yellow guidon rather intriguingly bears the combined arms of Robert Rich and his wife. The yellow ground might suggest the 8th Dragoons were it not for the fact that Rich transferred from that regiment to the 4th in 1735. Moreover the 8th (St. George's) Dragoons did not serve in Flanders. Unlikely though it may seem therefore Rich's 4th Dragoons may have been carrying this yellow guidon in 1745, losing both it and the green one illustrated elsewhere at Melle on 9 June 1745 where the regiment lost very heavily. The reverse of the guidon bears a rather old-fashioned doubled GR cypher. (Author)

3rd (King's Own) Dragoons

Light blue facings, waistcoat and breeches. Buff small-clothes 1768. Yellow lace with buttons set three and three. Red furniture, blue by 1768 with 'Royal' lace.

4th Dragoons

Pea-green facings (full green 1768), waistcoat and breeches. White lace with buttons set two and two. Green furniture, white lace with red stripe – changed to 'Royal' lace by 1790. Trumpeters all negroes 1776.

5th (Royal Irish) Dragoons

Blue facings, waistcoat and breeches. Yellow lace, but white by 1768 with buttons set three and three.

Two troops wearing grenadier caps as late as 1768. Said to have been a distinction conferred on the regiment in Queen Anne's time, but ordered to be discontinued 1769 in conformity with 1751 Warrant. Blue furniture with 'Royal' lace. Trumpeters on bays 1775.

6th (Inniskilling) Dragoons

'Full Yellow' facings, waistcoat and breeches. Yellow lace – white by 1768 with buttons set two and two. Yellow furniture, white lace with blue stripe. Trumpeters and farriers on greys 1777.

7th (Queen's) Dragoons

White facings, waistcoat and breeches. White lace with buttons set three and three. Converted to Light Dragoons 1783. Officers' sword belts noted to be worn under the jacket 1789 and 1790 – ordered to be worn outside. White furniture with 'Royal' lace.

8th Dragoons

Orange facings, waistcoat and breeches before 1748 and thereafter yellow. White lace with buttons set three and three. Orange, then yellow furniture, white lace with a yellow stripe. Apparently using goatskin furniture from c1787. Permitted to wear cross belts as a distinction from Queen Anne's war. This distinction was apparently lost when they converted to Light Dragoons in 1775.

9th Dragoons

Buff facings, waistcoat and breeches. White lace with buttons set two and two. Buff furniture, lace white with a blue stripe.

Officer's cap, Light Troop, 2nd Dragoons c1760. In contrast to the rather ambiguously decorated cap worn in 1742 this design, first seen in Morier's painting of 1748 is uncompromisingly Scottish in character. (Author)

10th Dragoons

Yellow facings, waistcoat and breeches. White lace with buttons set three, four and five. Yellow furniture, white lace with green stripe. Officers' swords in form of scimitars without guards to the hilt 1770. Light Dragoons 1783, but 1789 inspection comments on heavy dragoon furniture

11th Dragoons

White cuffs, buff linings, white waistcoat, red breeches – all buff by 1748. White lace, buttons set three and three. White linings reported 1776, but buff in the following year.

Buff furniture, white lace with green stripe. 1775 report noted that housings which had been made up in 1763 but not delivered until 1775 were moth-eaten. Trumpeters on greys 1777.

Light Dragoons 1783 – inspection report for following year comments on clothing being the same as worn when heavy dragoons, only cut shorter and still without lapels.

1789 inspection mentions old heavy dragoon

furniture still in use, and buff wings on shells – ordered to be discontinued 1790. Same inspection mentioned swords left on horses when regiment dismounted.

12th Dragoons

White facings and waistcoat, red breeches (white by 1748). On conversion to Light Dragoons (Prince of Wales) received black facings – including half-lapels. White lace with buttons set two and two. Originally white furniture but 1768 Warrant specifies 'black with stripes of white goatskin'. No lace.

13th Dragoons

Green cuffs, buff linings, white waistcoat and breeches – all light green by 1748. Buff small-clothes 1768. Facings also changed to buff on conversion to Light Dragoons in 1783. White lace, although officers had gold lace as early as 1751, but yellow lace specified in 1768. Buttons set three and three. Buff furniture, green by 1768, white lace with yellow stripe.

14th Dragoons

Pale or lemon yellow facings, white waistcoat and breeches – all pale yellow by 1748. Facings briefly changed to green on conversion to Light Dragoons in 1775. Yellow lace, white by 1768 with buttons set three and three.

Pale yellow furniture, white lace with red and green stripes. However, letter of March 1792 gives permission for change from black to yellow furniture. Trumpeters on greys 1775.

15th Dragoons (disb. 1748)

Green facings, buff waistcoat and breeches. Yellow lace. Green furniture.

15th King's Light Dragoons (raised 1759)

Green facings, white linings, waistcoats and breeches. White lace. Granted blue facings in 1766. Buttons set two and two.

Facings changed to red on adopting blue jackets in 1784. 1789 inspection mentions red wings on shells – ordered to be discontinued in the following year.

Black helmets with white fittings, initially green

turban and red mane. Sergeants originally had green sashes.

White furniture, originally edged white with red stripe, but edged with 'Royal' lace after 1766.

Trumpeters on greys 1777. Same inspection mentions swords left on horses when dismounted 'as is practised by the other Dragoon regiments'.

16th Queen's Light Dragoons

Black collar and cuffs, white linings. No lapels on coat, but white lace loops in threes. White waistcoat and breeches. Blue facings – including lapels granted in 1766. Buttons set two and two in 1768. White furniture with 'Royal' lace.

17th Light Dragoons

(No details are known of the uniform worn by the original 17th Dragoons raised but never completed in Scotland by Lord Aberdour. The regiment now known as the 17th was originally raised as the 18th Light Dragoons.)

White facings, waistcoat and breeches. Officers had blue cloaks lined white 1771.

Surviving first pattern helmet has a red front plate, edged with fur and bears a crossed bones badge over the skull. Subsequently skull and crossbones were joined with the skull on top. White turban mentioned in 1768 inspection. White furniture, white lace with black edge.

18th Light Dragoons

White facings, waistcoat and breeches – unauthorised scarlet edging to waistcoat noted in portraits and inspection reports. White lace with buttons set two and two. White furniture, red and white lace.

Hogarth's celebrated March of the Guards to Finchley. This is, no doubt, as exaggerated as most caricatures but nevertheless succeeds very well in conveying the often chaotic nature of military operations. (NMS)

A REPRESENTATION of the MARCH of the GUARDS towards SCOTLAND, in the YEAR 1745.

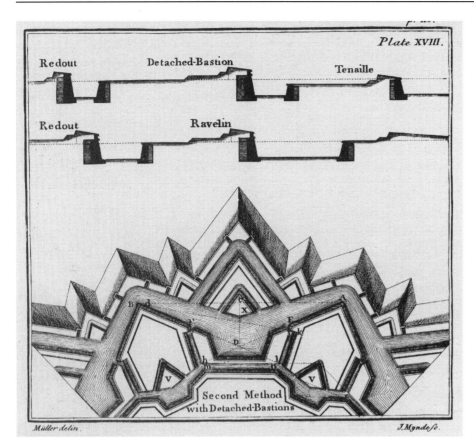

Eighteenth-century fortifications as depicted in Muller's 'Elements of Fortification'. As far as the British Army was concerned the standard work upon the subject in English. (Author's collection)

19th Light Dragoons (raised 1779 – disbanded 1783)
Green facings, white small-clothes.

19th Light Dragoons (1783-)
See 23rd Light Dragoons.

20th Light Dragoons (raised 1779 – disbanded 1783)
Yellow facings, white small-clothes.

20th (Jamaica) Light Dragoons (raised 1792)
Dark blue jacket with yellow facings. Tin helmet with horsehair mane and alligator badge on front.

21st Light Dragoons (Royal Foresters) (disbanded 1763)
See text accompanying plate C3.

21st Light Dragoons (raised 1779 – disbanded 1783)
White facings and small-clothes.

22nd Light Dragoons (disbanded 1763)
No details known but possibly black facings.

22nd Light Dragoons (raised 1779 – disbanded 1783)
Green jackets.

23rd Light Dragoons (raised 1779)
Red coats with green facings and white small clothes. Buttons looped two and two. Apparently went out to India wearing green jackets. By virtue of serving there escaped disbandment in 1783 and redesignated 19th Light Dragoons. Facings changed to yellow 1786.

THE BOARD OF ORDNANCE

The Board had a variety of functions in the 18th century, including the supply of guns and ammunition to the Royal Navy as well as to the army. In very general terms it was responsible for supplying the various forces of the crown with all the lethal and non-lethal hardware which they required (including powder, cannon and small arms for the navy), for training and administering the Royal Artillery (including the quite separate Irish Artillery raised in 1755) and Engineers. From there it was a short step to supplying fortifications and, increasingly, purpose-built barracks.

As an organisation it was also, in theory, quite independent and its officers and men were not, strictly speaking, part of the army. Officers received their commissions from the Board, not from the crown. In this respect they were rather like the officers and men of the navy and marines who answered to the Board of Admiralty rather than the King.

This relationship could at times produce some curious anomalies. In the early days, it was common for engineer officers to simultaneously hold military commissions in regiments of the line – and commoner still for regimental officers to fill in as engineers when Woolwich trained personnel were wanting. Indeed, in 1772 Thomas Simes, *The Military Guide for Young Officers* specifically recommended that newly commissioned infantry officers should furnish themselves with a copy of John Muller's 1746 treatise on fortification, but said nothing about other books. Moreover although an Army officer receiving half pay could not serve at the same time in another regiment of the line or even in the militia as these were 'offices of profit under the crown' there was nothing whatever to prevent his working for the Board of Ordnance and drawing his half pay at the same time.

Although the Board's independence could be quite jealously guarded on occasion, it was little exercised in the field. The most obvious distinction was the wearing of blue coats by the King's artillerymen. Curiously enough this sartorial distinction was not extended to the Board's engineer officers until 1782. Until that time they wore red coats, perhaps as a hangover from the days when they also held infantry commissions but more likely to make them less conspicuous. The necessity for close reconnaissance of fortified places made the engineer's job dangerous enough without drawing attention to himself unnecessarily. Having changed to Ordnance blue in 1782,

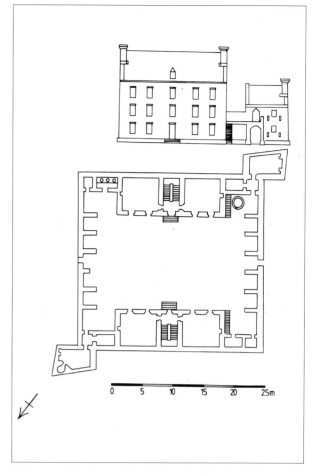

In practice the army's fortifications were often much less elaborate than those described by Muller and other experts. This is a plan of Ruthven barracks, built in 1719-21 and successfully defended by Sergeant Terry Molloy and a dozen men in 1745. It was originally hoped to build four flanking towers (one hesitates to describe them as bastions) 'if the money answers' – very evidently it did not. (Author)

the Engineers reverted to red in 1811 precisely for that very reason, having suffered very high casualties in the Peninsula.

The real distinction between King's officers and Ordnance officers lay in the system of training and promotion. Due to the technical nature of the service, the Board's officers could not purchase their commissions and promotion was entirely a matter of seniority. Moreover while the training, if any, received by the young infantry or cavalry officer was a matter for his regiment, the Board's officers were trained in the intricacies of their craft at Woolwich, and just as importantly

received 'hands on' experience as Cadet Matrosses (unskilled labourers), Cadet Gunners and Cadet Fireworkers (Corporals) before gaining their commissions.

The four battalions of Royal Artillery, and the quite separate Royal Irish Artillery, were purely administrative units. The basic unit was the company and the one commanded by Captain Lieutenant John Godwin at Culloden was perhaps typical in comprising ten officers, a number of volunteers and 106 NCOs and men. Between them they were responsible for looking after ten 3lb cannon and six Coehorn mortars.

This particular artillery train had been assembled specifically for operations in Scotland and generally speaking the Royal Artillery displayed considerable flexibility in providing the appropriate weight of artillery support for a particular operation. This could vary, according to circumstances, from a single curricle gun and a couple of gunner/instructors, to two or more 'brigades' of artillery. At Minden for example the Royal Artillery mustered a brigade of nine light guns under Captain Foy and nine heavy (12-pounders) under Captain MacBean.

THE PLATES

Plate A: Regular Cavalry 1740s
A1: Trooper, 2nd (Royal North British) Dragoons 1748

The 2nd Dragoons, better known as the Scots Greys, had a solidly impressive combat record during the reign of King George II. In 1742 they were ordered to Flanders and served there until the cessation of hostilities in 1748. In 1745, they were one of only six cavalry regiments left there during the Jacobite emergency. During the Seven Years War, they served in Germany, led by the eccentric Lieutenant Colonel George Preston, who insisted on wearing a 17th-century buffcoat in action.

This figure is based primarily upon Morier's painting of a soldier of the regiment c1748, and a surviving coat in the Scottish United Services Museum. With the obvious exception of the headgear the characteristics of the uniform were common to all dragoon regiments. The coat is double-breasted and unlaced. By 1753, only the 2nd and 3rd Regiments of Dragoons were wearing

buttons and holes on both sides of the coat and in January of that year they were both ordered to fall into line with the other regiments who by then were wearing single-breasted coats.

Thin white lace binding appeared on the buttonholes by 1748, but otherwise the only real decorative feature is the shoulder-knot worn on the right. The elaborate version worn by officers is said to represent the points or ties on a knightly arming doublet, but it is questionable whether those worn by troopers of dragoons did so. Since troopers ranked with infantry corporals, the shoulder knot may simply have been a method of displaying that equality. Another notable distinguishing feature of cavalry uniform (apart from the boots) was the fact that while infantrymen invariably wore red waistcoats, and with the exception of Royal regiments, had red breeches too. Cavalrymen wore small-clothes of the regimental facing colour – in this case blue – or else a neutral white or buff. Similarly while all but a handful of infantry units wore plain white lace on their hats, irrespective of whether their officers

Culloden Moor as depicted by Bowles. The grouping of the Duke of Cumberland and his staff in the central foreground is done purely for dramatic effect, but otherwise the print usefully depicts General Hawley's cavalry breaking through the Culwhiniac enclosures on the left and on the right Barrell's 4th Foot receiving the rebels with bayonets charged breast high. Intriguingly one of the rebels can just be seen with his hand on Barrell's colours – an oblique reference to the temporary loss of one. (NMS)

wore silver or gold lace, in the cavalry white or yellow lace was used as appropriate.

Apart from their caps, this regiment was famously distinguished by its grey horses – hence the 'Scots Greys' nickname – and also by wearing white accoutrements, 20 years before the rest of the army.

The grenadier cap worn by this regiment instead of the usual tricorne hat appears to have changed between 1742 and 1748. *The Cloathing Book* version featured a red front embroidered strangely enough with the red cross of St. George within the garter, superimposed on a white star. The frontlet is blue with a thistle and *NEMO ME*

William Augustus, Duke of Cumberland (1721-1765) at Culloden by David Morier. Cumberland was one of the most able and influential commanders of the British Army in the 18th century. In this important portrait he wears a scarlet coat faced with very dark blue and lavish quantities of gold braid. The saddle housings are also red and gold and interestingly enough do not include separate holster caps. The infantry battalion in the middle distance has yellow facings and appears to represent Pulteney's 13th Foot. Close examination reveals that both officers and men are wearing back gaiters. (NMS)

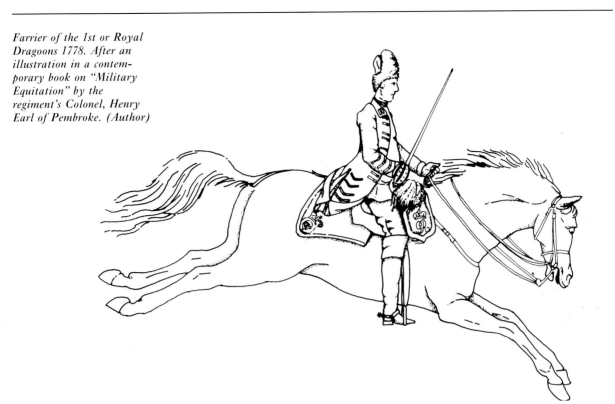

Farrier of the 1st or Royal Dragoons 1778. After an illustration in a contemporary book on "Military Equitation" by the regiment's Colonel, Henry Earl of Pembroke. (Author)

IMPUNE LACESSIT on a white lapel. The rear of the cap is red over blue and the whole is piped in yellow. By 1748 however the design, as shown, was much more Scottish in character and is not unlike that displayed on the grenadier caps of the 21st Foot. In the 1750s if not before, waterproof oilskin covers were worn over the caps in foul weather. Black bearskin caps were authorised in 1768, bearing the same badge on the front.

Like their infantry counterparts, cavalrymen also had forage caps (called for the sake of distinction watering caps). These were red with a hanging hood, or bag, and a small frontlet of the regimental facing colour, bearing its number on it. Gaiters were also supposed to be worn by Dragoons when dismounted.

A2: Officer, 2nd (Montagu's) Dragoon Guards c1747

Montagu's 2nd Horse, not to be confused with the short-lived 9th Horse raised during the Jacobite emergency, was a good solid regiment. Like both the other regiments of Horse on the English establishment it was converted into Dragoon Guards in 1746. Based on a portrait of

an unknown officer, this figure usefully illustrates some of the differences between the uniforms of dragoons and heavy cavalry.

The principal and most obvious difference is the presence of lapels on the coat. All regiments of Horse had worn rather old-fashioned lapels which were quite narrow and extended the full length of the coat from the neck to the hem – despite the fact that even as early as 1742 troopers wore their coat skirts hooked back. By way of a distinction, those regiments converted into Dragoon Guards adopted infantry-style half-lapels. As Horse, they had worn two cross-belts – a broad carbine belt over the left shoulder and an equally broad baldric or sword-belt over the right shoulder. On becoming Dragoon Guards, however, they adopted Dragoon accoutrements comprising a substantial waistbelt for the sword and a cartouche box and sling over the left shoulder. Oddly enough on the other hand, one Dragoon regiment, the 8th, bore their swords in a baldric instead of a waistbelt. This, according to General Severne who was Colonel of the regiment from 1760 to 1787, was a distinction gained at the battle of Almenara in 1710, when they had

Heavy cavalry officer, c1780. After a caricature published by Bowles and Carter. The regiment is unidentified but the carbine belt suggests one of the troops of Lifeguards.

captured a Spanish regiment of Horse and appropriated their belts. At any rate all accoutrements were invariably yellowish buff coloured at this period, as indeed were the troopers' gauntlets – the only exception being the white accoutrements of the 2nd Dragoons.

A3: Farrier, 11th (Kerr's) Dragoons 1748

Originally raised in Scotland and still by this period largely officered by Scots, Lord Mark Kerr's 11th Dragoons were one of the better cavalry regiments and distinguished themselves at Culloden in 1746 by forcing their way across a heavily defended re-entrant to get into the Jacobite rear. The 1742 *Cloathing Book* shows them wearing the white facings which appear to have been characteristic of Scots regiments before and for some years after the Union in 1707. But by 1748 when they were painted by Morier their facings had changed to buff, an alteration confirmed in the subsequent Royal Warrant of 1751.

Like the pioneers borne on the strength of infantry battalions, farriers were at once tradesmen and perhaps paradoxically were invariably some of the more impressive figures on parade, marching with their axes displayed. The purpose of the axe was a means both for dispatching wounded animals and for recovering the hoof branded with the animal's regimental number. Lacking such proof that a horse had been lost on service it was extremely difficult for the regiment to recover the cost from the government.

His uniform is quite unusual. He wears a fur cap. But while trumpeters and drummers wore the customary reversed clothing and infantry pioneers were distinguished only by their caps and aprons, farriers wore blue coats turned up with the regimental facing colour. This distinction did not however extend to the cloak, which was an ordinary trooper's red one, lined in the regimental facing colour. In 1768, the coats appear to have been modified slightly in that all were to have blue linings and where appropriate blue lapels as well. Only the collar and cuffs were to be of the facing colour, with the exception of Royal regiments which had red ones instead of their customary blue. At the same time all farriers were also put into blue waistcoats and breeches.

Apart from the axe, Morier shows the farrier to be unarmed and the only visible accoutrement is a small case for the axe, carried on a fairly narrow sling. The pistol holsters on the front of the saddle were also replaced by churns or cylindrical leather panniers carrying horse-shoes and nails. This would indicate that the farrier was intended

Regular Cavalry 1740s
1: Trooper, 2nd (Royal North British) Dragoons, 1748
2: Officer, 2nd (Montagu's) Dragoon Guards, c1747
3: Farrier, 11th (Kerr's) Dragoons, 1748

A

The Jacobite Emergency 1745/6
1: Trooper, Duke of Cumberland's Hussar's
2: Private Gentleman, Yorkshire Hunters
3: Private, Georgia Rangers

B

The Seven Years War
1: Sergeant, Light Troop 2nd Dragoons, 1756
2: Officer, 13th (Douglas') Dragoons, 1767
3: Trooper, 21st Light Dragoons (Royal Foresters), 1760

2

3

1

The American War of Independence
1: Private, Light Infantry Troop, 16th Light Dragoons
2: Sergeant, 17th Light Dragoons, 1776
3: Trooper, Castleknock Horse, 1779

D

1: Officer, 7th Dragoons, 1770
2: Trooper, 16th Light Dragoons, 1790
3: Captain Alexander Grant, Madras Governor's Bodyguard

E

Royal Artillery
1: Forbes MacBean, 1748
2: Gunner, Royal Artillery, 1748
3: Conductor, 1748

F

1: Gunner, 4th Battalion Royal Artillery, 1777
2: Officer, Corps of Engineers, 1778
3: Military Artificer, 1786

G

1: Officer, Royal Artillery, 1794
2: Gunner, 2/Madras Artillery, 1790
3: Gunner, Invalid Battalion, Royal Artillery, 1793

H

Sir John Burgoyne (1723-1792). Entered the army as a sub-brigadier in the Horse Guards 1737, Cornet 1st Royal Dragoons 1744-1751. Re-entered army as Captain 11th Dragoons, Captain Lieutenant 2nd Footguards 1758, Lieutenant Colonel commandant of his own 16th Light Dragoons 1759 and subsequently promoted to full Colonel 1763. Major General 1772, sent to Boston 1775 and to Canada in the following year. Intrigued his way into command of expedition to Albany in the following year but led it to disaster at Saratoga. Although not without ability his various appointments were all achieved through influence, intrigue and purchase. (Author's collection)

involved were regulars, but they also included some rather unusual units. One brigade, commanded by Major General Humphrey Bland, was made up of his own 3rd Dragoons, Cobham's 10th and Kerr's 11th Dragoons. The second brigade was considerably less conventional in its composition. It was made up of St. George's 8th Dragoons, Montagu's 3rd Horse, the blue-coated Yorkshire Hunters and the green-jacketed Georgia Rangers.

After an initial skirmish largely involving units of Oglethorpe's Brigade, Cumberland, who was taking personal charge of the operation, ordered Bland's brigade to dismount and attack the Jacobite rearguard under cover of darkness. The rebels promptly counter-attacked. In the fight which followed six men of Bland's 3rd Dragoons were killed, three of Cobham's 10th and one of Kerr's 11th, besides four officers of Bland's were wounded along with an unknown number of men. Jacobite losses were said to have been comparable and the night ended in a draw with the Dragoons left in possession of the field and the rebels getting clean away.

to be a non-combatant, no doubt because on campaign a good one was very hard to replace. Nevertheless it is interesting that a farrier of the 1st (Royal) Dragoons is depicted in a later drawing going over a jump with his sword in his hand.

Plate B: *The Jacobite Emergency 1745/6*

As the Jacobites retreated from Derby in December 1745 the British Army made strenuous efforts to intercept them before they managed to reach the Scottish border. Two cavalry brigades eventually made contact at Clifton Moor on the afternoon of the 18th and a lengthy rearguard action commenced. Most of the cavalry units

Major John Andre depicted in the uniform of an Aide de Camp. (Author's collection)

Light Dragoon officer, c1780. After a caricature published by Bowles and Carter. The regiment is unidentified but the chief point of interest in this figure is his wearing of short gaiters instead of boots while dismounted. This order of dress is often referred to but rarely illustrated. (Author's collection)

B1: Trooper, Duke of Cumberland's Hussars

This small unit primarily existed as the Duke of Cumberland's personal bodyguard but were evidently not averse to getting involved in any fighting. A volunteer surgeon with Bland's brigade

afterwards wrote, 'As the Horse was coming off Clifton Moor into the town, our Hussars and Rangers engag'd all the Rebel Hussars, who were headed by one Captain Hamilton..... he was cut down and taken by one of the Duke's Hussars, after a stout resistance.'

At least one other contemporary account refers to the hussar in question as being an Austrian which may mean that they were, in fact, Hungarians. The detachment is also known to have fought at Culloden, on 16 April 1746, where one of them was credited (wrongly) with capturing one of the rebel leaders, Lord Kilmarnock.

This reconstruction is based on some rather small figures painted by David Morier. The green and crimson uniform is the Duke's personal livery and although the basic outline conforms to the traditional 'Hungarian' pattern, there are some interesting peculiarities such as the dragoon style boots, the unbraided jacket worn in place of a dolman, and the rather long pelisse.

B2: Private Gentleman, Yorkshire Hunters

The Hunters were a volunteer unit raised in September 1745: 'Several Gentlemen of considerable Fortunes have resolved to form themselves and their Servants, into a Regiment of Light Horse for the King's Service. Such as compose it are to be mounted on stout Fox Hunters and are to serve at their own expence, under the Command of the Hon. Major General Oglethorpe. They were on this day (30 September) muster'd upon a place called Knavesmire, and made a very fine Appearance. The Gentlemen who composed the first Rank, were all dress'd in Blue, trimm'd with Scarlet, and Gold Buttons, Gold Lac'd Hats, Light Boots and Saddles &c. their Arms were short Bullet Guns slung, Pistols of a moderate size, and strong plain Swords. The second and third Ranks, which were made up of their Servants, were dress'd in Blue, with Brass Buttons, their Accoutrements all light and serviceable, with short Guns and Pistols, and each with a Pole-axe in his hand.'

The reference to 'short Bullet guns slung' is rather puzzling as carbines at this period normally had 42-inch barrels, and it is just possible that they actually had blunderbusses. At any rate a

subsequent description of their arrival in Doncaster on 20 October makes no mention of the pole-axes, but does add the curious detail that they all wore green cockades. This distinction may have been a compliment to General Oglethorpe, the nominal commander of the unit, whose own regular regiment had green facings.

B3: Private, Georgia Rangers

Brigadier General James Oglethorpe was Governor of the colony of Georgia and Colonel of the 42nd Foot, a regular battalion raised specifically for the defence of the colony. It was 'broke' in 1748 and reformed as three independent companies. In 1745, Oglethorpe was in England recruiting both for his infantry regiment and a green-jacketed mounted infantry unit attached to it called the Georgia Rangers. (Frustratingly, the Commission Registers fail to distinguish between officers appointed to the two units.) On the point of embarkation when the rebellion broke out the Rangers were diverted to Hull and attached to General Wade's army assembling at Newcastle.

A very atmospheric 19th-century evocation of a siege battery at Yorktown in 1781. Although the gunners can be identified as French by their moustaches, a British gun emplacement would have looked remarkably similar. (Author's collection)

Oglethorpe's 42nd Foot wore the usual red coats with green facings but less is known of his Rangers and contemporary accounts refer only to a green uniform and leather cap. Although this particular individual is wearing infantry-style gaiters, it is probable that most Rangers wore boots as their intended role was to patrol the Georgia coastline, looking out for Spanish raiders.

The most exotic member of this unusual unit was mentioned in a tantalisingly offhand report from Brough in January 1746: 'On Saturday last Gen. Oglethorpe and his Lady, and his Georgia Rangers, with the Indian King and Queen &c. passed over Stainmoor on their road to York.' History, alas, does not record whether the Indian 'King' and his attendants were painted for battle at Clifton.

Light Dragoons (probably Provincials) wearing Tarleton helmets get in amongst an American battery. (Author's collection)

Plate C: The Seven Years War
C1: Sergeant, Light Troop, 2nd Dragoons 1756
In 1756, a Light Troop was added to the establishment of all three regiments of Dragoon Guards and the Dragoon regiments then carried on the English Establishment. In practice they served detached, grouped like the flank companies of infantry regiments into *ad hoc* squadrons. While most of the Greys were serving with some distinction in Germany their Light Troop took part in the coastal raids against St Malo and Cherbourg.

The men recruited for these Troops were to be 'light, active young men' mounted on 'well turned nimble road horses'. Light jockey boots with stiff tops and leather caps were prescribed but otherwise they were to wear the uniform of their parent corps. The caps were to have turned-up fronts bearing the Royal cypher and regimental number, and a brass crest on the skull. Apart from

the number, the only regimental distinction authorised was a horsehair tufts, half and half red and the unit's facing colour.

Rather predictably most units arranged matters to their own satisfaction. A painting by Morier shows a trooper of the 11th Dragoons wearing a cap with a red front, edged with brass, and an all white tuft. Not surprisingly the 2nd Dragoons' cap was more distinctive still. Effectively the regulation leather cap was covered by a smaller version of the grenadier cap peculiar to this regiment. Apart from size this differed from the normal version only in lacking the red 'bag' at the rear – thus exposing the brass-crested skull – and having a red, white and blue horsehair plume at the side.

Saddlery, weapons and accoutrements were suitably lightened and included a new carbine with a 36-inch barrel in place of the normal 42-inch barrel version, a single pistol and a straight-bladed sword. Although Kingston's 10th Horse raised in 1745 and disbanded in 1748 as Cumberland's 15th Dragoons had carried swords with curved blades, straight-bladed weapons seem to have been pretty universal in British service for most of the 18th century. Accoutrements were supposed to be made from tanned rather than buff leather, but there is no doubt that the Greys once again contrived to whiten theirs.

C2: Officer, 13th (Douglas's) Dragoons 1767

The 13th were an all too typical product of the inefficient Irish Establishment. Raised in 1715 their Colonels included good soldiers such as Henry Hawley (1730-1740) and Humphrey Bland (1741-1743). But they failed dismally when committed to action in the Jacobite Rising of 1745. By that time they were commanded by a Scots professional soldier, James Gardiner and promptly abandoned him to his fate at Prestonpans. They also ran away at Falkirk some months later. As soon as the emergency was over they were quietly returned to the obscurity of the Irish Establishment from whence they had come in 1743. This reconstruction is based on a portrait by Pompeo Batoni of Captain James Stewart of Killymoon. The uniform, conforming to both the 1742 *Cloathing Book* and 1751 Warrant, shows how cavalry units wearing the same facing colours were distinguished. In this case the buttons and gold braid loops are arranged in three, and white small-clothes are worn instead of the green waistcoat and breeches worn by Rich's 4th Dragoons. Stewart's portrait appears to depict silk small-clothes, explicable perhaps by his wearing the uniform on a social occasion rather than on duty. This impression is reinforced by his wearing stockings and shoes rather than riding boots. But otherwise his uniform conforms to regulations.

C3: Trooper, 21st Light Dragoons (Royal Foresters) 1760

When the experiment of raising Light Troops for existing Dragoon regiments proved successful, the logical step was to raise complete regiments. The first and most spectacularly successful of these was the 15th, who distinguished themselves at Emsdorf. Others soon followed. Perhaps the most interesting was Granby's 21st Light Dragoons, otherwise known as the Royal Foresters. Although Granby himself could take little more than a proprietorial interest in the regiment since he was otherwise fully engaged in commanding the

Sir William Howe (1729-1814). Entered army as Cornet 15th (Cumberland's) Dragoons 1746, Lieutenant 1747, Captain 20th Foot 1750, Major 60th 1756, Lieutenant Colonel 58th 1757, Colonel 46th 1764. Major General 1772 and commander-in-chief North America 1775-1778, being promoted to Lieutenant General in 1777. Colonel 23rd Foot 1775-1786, then 19th Light Dragoons until his death. Promotions and appointments were managed through his connections (being a half cousin of the King helped) nevertheless he was an able strategist who quite literally ran rings around George Washington. Nevertheless he lacked the killer instinct necessary to press home his victories. (Author's collection)

British contingent in Germany, the regiment was generally agreed to be a first class one reflecting the very latest and best continental practice. Indeed Captain Robert Hinde, author of the influential *Discipline of the Light Horse* (1778), served in the regiment. Unfortunately it was destined never to see action as a unit although a number of men were drafted into units serving in Germany. Strangely enough a solitary officer of the Royal Foresters was included in the prisoners taken by the Americans at Yorktown in 1781 – eighteen years after the regiment was disbanded!

The uniform is depicted by Morier and particularly noteworthy is the German-style helmet with the rather curiously shaped frontlet – a form usually associated with Hessian troops. Officers' helmets were edged with fur. All of the new regiments of Light Dragoons wore lapels on their coats and in this particular case the horse fur-

Guidon, Horse Grenadier Guards c1780. Crimson with lavish gold embroidery and fringing. (Author)

niture was also unusual in comprising a large hussar style shabraque of white goatskin for rank and file, and white bearskin for officers. The latter were edged with wolf-toothed silver braid (with a blue silk line running down the middle) and all ranks had a blue badge over the holsters, bearing the regimental number and royal cypher picked out in white or silver.

Plate D. The American War of Independence
D1: Private, *Light Infantry Troop, 16th Light Dragoons*
Lieutenant Colonel John Burgoyne (as he then was) received Letters of Service to raise the 16th Light Dragoons on 4 August 1759. Two troops took part in the Belle-Ile expedition in 1761 and the following year the whole regiment sailed for Portugal. In 1766, they became the Queen's Dragoons and adopted blue facings in place of the original black ones. At the same time a badge comprising the Queen's cypher within the garter was placed on their helmets. One of two cavalry regiments sent to America, their six mounted troops were augmented by a seventh, dismounted one in 1776.

'These were provided with a loose cloak or mantle instead of the cloak, which they carry over their knapsack. They are not provided with boots but have brown cloth gaiters. They have no broadswords, have a leather helmet a good deal like that of the Light Infantry. Each man carries a hatchet. They act separately as Light Infantry.'

It might be tempting to view this experiment as a move in the direction of the 'legion' organisation which had already proved popular on the continent and which would soon be widely adopted by both the Loyalist and Colonial provincial units. However the proportion of horse to foot (the dismounted troop had a strength of only 29 men) suggests that the true purpose of this formation was not to act as an integrated combat unit, but in fact to provide local security for the regiment's quarters and foraging parties.

In 1778, the regiment was ordered home and in accordance with the usual practice only the officers and senior NCOs actually embarked, the effective rank and file being turned over to the 17th Light Dragoons. Then the Light Infantry Troop appears to have been disbanded.

D2: Sergeant, 17th Light Dragoons 1776

Raised in 1759 as the 18th Light Dragoons by Colonel John Hale, this regiment became the 17th in 1763. (The original 17th Light Dragoons, a Scottish unit commanded by Lord Aberdour, was never completed.) Traditionally, the 'scalped face and shinbones' badge is said to have been worn in remembrance of General Wolfe. Although this is quite possible it is rather more likely that the actual inspiration was the very similar badge worn by the famous Black Hussars in the Prussian service. It is uncertain just how long this particular style of helmet continued to be worn. A 1784 drawing by Bunbury shows another sergeant of this or another regiment with white facings wearing a Tarleton Helmet.

Like the 16th, this regiment was sent to America in 1775 and served there with some distinction throughout the war, mainly in the north – a small party was even present at Bunker Hill. A better known detachment later served in the south where they provided some badly needed stiffening for Banastre Tarleton's rather undisciplined British Legion. Oddly enough, this provincial corps was originally raised by an officer of the 17th named Cathcart. Despite this connection the detachment resisted all Tarleton's attempts to have them drafted into the Legion after it was taken on to the regular establishment in June 1781.

D3: Trooper, Castleknock Horse 1779

The despatch of considerable numbers of troops from Ireland to America aroused fears of a repeat of Thurot's virtually unopposed descent on Carrickfergus in 1760. A lack of funds prevented the implementation of the 1778 Militia Act, but instead a volunteer movement sprang into existence. Originally, it had no object beyond the immediate defence of the country, but this soon changed and the volunteers threw their weight behind pressure for the repeal of the infamous Poyning's Act, a medieval statute which subjected all Irish legislation to ratification by the English Parliament. The growing politicisation of the volunteers eventually led to their suppression in 1793. Paradoxically however, although some of the members went on to found the United Irishmen, the vast majority of the volunteers went on to

Sir Henry Clinton. Howe's successor as commander-in-chief North America, he had been a more than capable subordinate but lacked the self-confidence necessary for independent command. (Author's collection)

represent the Protestant ascendancy.

This trooper is reconstructed from a painting by Wheatley depicting a parade of volunteers on College Green in Dublin, on 4 November 1779, celebrating the birthday of King William III – which is a pretty good indicator of their real political sympathies. The uniform, and particularly the helmet, is very French in style.

E1: Officer, 7th Dragoons 1770

The Royal Warrant of 1768 did little to alter the uniforms of dragoon regiments. Only the 12th, 15th, 16th, 17th and 18th were designated as Light Dragoons and distinguished from the 'Heavy' Dragoon regiments by the wearing of lapels on their coats and the substitution of

Officer of Light Dragoons (probably 16th) after Bunbury. Note the very long fur trimmed shell or 'kitt'. (Author)

helmets for cocked hats. The 7th were not converted to Light Dragoons until 1783.

This officer, based on a portrait, still wears the, by now, rather old-fashioned single breasted coat. The 7th were supposed to have white facings but the portrait shows a distinct buff tinge to both facings and small-clothes. It is also notable that the riding boots are now much lighter and less clumsy than those worn before.

E2: Trooper, 16th Light Dragoons 1790

In the aftermath of the American War there was a wide-ranging review of the army's uniforms and equipment. A number of changes were recommended, but the most dramatic alteration was seen in the clothing of Light Dragoons. The old long-tailed red coat was abandoned and replaced by a short single breasted round jacket in hussar style. There appears to have been an initial move in favour of a plain green jacket as previously worn by some Provincial cavalry units, and the 23rd Light Dragoons appear to have gone to India wearing them even though their uniform was actually supposed to be a red coat turned up with green.

The eventual choice, however, ordered in 1784, was for a dark blue hussar style dolman, braided with white cords. A second, sleeveless jacket or shell was worn on top, presumably for the sake of warmth. At the same time, the boots were lightened still further and the Tarleton helmet was officially authorised. The popularity of this new uniform may be gauged by the fact that, with the exception of the shell, it survived virtually unaltered until 1812.

This reconstruction is based on surviving items of clothing and a painting by Wheatley. The 16th had worn blue facings on the old red uniform, but when ordered into the new blue uniform the facings were changed to red. A sketch by Bunbury shows that the officers of the regiment wore rather long, Hungarian-style shells (which were apparently referred to as 'kitts') and that between 1785 and 1788 they had them rather dashingly lined with leopardskin. On 14 June 1788, all regiments of Light Dragoons were ordered to be dressed in the same uniforms and to be distinguished only by the facing colour on the collar and cuffs.

This order provoked an immediate protest from the 16th Dragoons and on 22 June the Adjutant General wrote rather apologetically to the regimental colonel, Major General Harcourt: 'The only object of this new order is to introduce a greater uniformity in the dress of the Light Cavalry Corps, than there was before. His Majesty therefore hoped you would not regret the exchanging the leopard skin lining of your Officers' uniforms, for that which is now ordered to be worn by all the officers of all the other Light Dragoon Regiments.'

E3: Captain Alexander Grant, Madras Governor's Bodyguard

Despite maintaining a solid core of European infantry and artillery units, the East India Company came to rely almost entirely upon native cavalry units with a few British officers. There were however occasional attempts to raise European cavalry units. Perhaps the most notable was a 'foreign legion' raised by a Swiss officer named Abraham Bonjour in 1768. This comprised a company of light infantry and a troop of hussars – the latter being, for the most part, French veterans who had originally come out to India with the Hussards de Conflans. The light infantry were to wear: 'a light jacket of green, faced with red, and a cap...They should have breeches and stockings all in one with black gaiters'.

No mention was made of the Hussars' dress but as Conflans' regiment also wore green faced with red (and red breeches) it would seem quite possible that Bonjour's troopers were still wearing their old French Army uniforms. The Hussars were dismounted in 1769 and the rest of the legion disbanded in 1769. The Company also had a troop of Dragoons in the early days of the Madras Army. But although favourably reviewed this was broken up in 1777, briefly reinstated and eventually disbanded in 1779.

The native cavalry regiments which replaced this rather raffish crew wore uniforms very closely patterned after European styles. This figure is based upon a representation of Captain Alexander Grant (1763-1801) in a well known painting by Home depicting the capture of Bangalore in 1791. Grant's background was typical of many EIC officers. He was the son of Ludovick Grant, minister of Ardchattan in Invernessshire. Commissioned a cornet in the Company's service on 19 June 1783 and a lieutenant in January 1786. The date of his captaincy is uncertain but he was promoted to Major in September 1799.

Apart from the fact that his jacket is scarlet rather than blue Captain Grant is distinguished as an EIC officer rather than a British regular only by his leopardskin sabretache, worn high up on the hip. A native trooper or Sowar standing beside Captain Grant in the Bangalore painting wears a very similar uniform to that shown here

Charles, Earl Cornwallis (1738-1805). A Guardsman like a great many other general officers he is best known for his southern campaign during the American War which culminated in the disastrous defeat at Yorktown in 1781. Despite this he went on to rebuild his career by serving as Governor General and commander-in-chief in India 1786-1793, Lord Lieutenant and commander-in-chief Ireland 1798-1801 and again Governor General of India in 1805. His appointments appear to reflect his well-attested popularity rather than any great ability. (Author's collection)

although the jacket is worn open from the throat to the belly and instead of a Tarleton helmet he wears a fairly tall pinkish red turban.

Plate F: Royal Artillery
F1: Forbes MacBean 1748

It was far from uncommon to find officers of relatively humble origins serving in the British Army during the 18th century. However, lacking money and influence few of them advanced far beyond the rank of captain, except in the Royal Artillery where seniority, and to a lesser extent merit, counted for everything. A notable example was Forbes MacBean, the son of an Inverness minister and step-brother of Lieutenant William Bannatyne

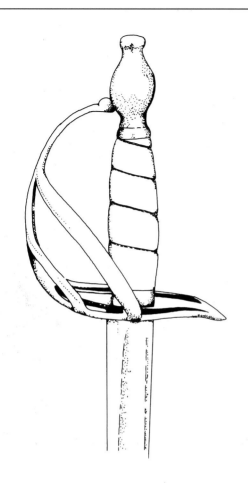

1788 pattern heavy cavalry sword. Prior to 1788 there was no regulation pattern and regimental colonels were free to equip their men as they pleased. Neither this weapon nor the 1788 pattern light cavalry sabre proved to be satisfactory and both were replaced in 1796. (Author)

(see MAA 285) and Captain Robert Bannatyne (see MAA 289). Entering the Royal Artillery as a Cadet Matross on 3 August 1743, he commanded two guns at Fontenoy in 1745, and later that year again served under Cumberland at the siege of Carlisle. For some reason he did not serve in Scotland, but at Lauffeldt and Rocoux he commanded the battalion guns attached to the 19th Foot. Promoted to Captain in January 1759 MacBean commanded a heavy artillery brigade using ten 12-pounders at Minden with some effect. In 1762 he went with the British expedition to Portugal and subsequently served as a colonel in the Portuguese Army between 1765 and 1768. Posted to Canada between 1769 and 1773 he returned there as CRA (Commander Royal

Artillery) in succession to Major General Phillips in 1778. This brought him a well merited promotion to lieutenant colonel in 1782 and then the appointment of Colonel Commandant of the Invalid Battalion in 1793. Promotion to Major General followed almost at once and active to the end he died a Lieutenant General at Woolwich in 1800. One of the Royal Artillery's more intellectual officers, MacBean was elected a Fellow of the Royal Society in 1786.

This reconstruction is largely based on a painting by David Morier, depicting the train of artillery encamped at Roermond in Holland in 1748. MacBean wears the traditional gunner's uniform of a dark blue coat faced with red, but is distinguished from the rank and file by his red waistcoat and breeches. The wearing of white gaiters in the field is extremely unusual and presumably reflects the fact that the artillery train was then at rest.

F2: Gunner, Royal Artillery 1748
The 1742 *Cloathing Book* depicted a very plain uniform without any lace and rather short 'half-lapels'. C.C.P. Lawson quotes a 1750 order that sergeants' coats were to be laced with gold and the other NCOs with yellow worsted. This might suggest that the gunners's coats were still unlaced at this date. But Morier's painting which can be positively dated to the spring of 1748 clearly shows lace worn by all ranks. This gunner, taken from the painting, displays a number of other interesting features. His gaiters are black as would be expected on campaign and in contrast to the red small-clothes worn by his officers this man wears blue. A rather curiously shaped belly-box and black bayonet-frog is carried on a thin belt around his waist. In 1742, gunners and matrosses were supposed to be armed with linstocks – combination spears and slow-match holders. A 1749 order directed these to be laid aside in favour of carbines and bayonets, but once again Morier's painting shows this order to have been widely anticipated. Those carbines carried during the 1740s were presumably the same 42-inch barrel weapons issued to dragoons, but in 1757 a cheaper version specifically intended for issue to artillerymen was set up. The buff sling supports a

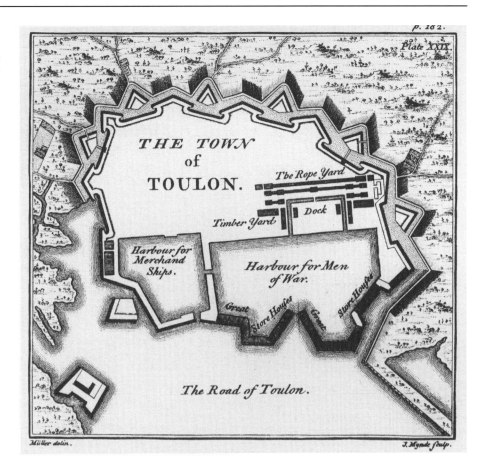

Map of the defences of Toulon from Muller's **Elements of Fortification** *This particular illustration was no doubt studied with great interest during the Allied occupation of the port in 1794.*

large powder-horn on his right hip. At the Court of Inquiry held into the débâcle at Prestonpans in September 1745, General Cope's CRA, Major Eaglefield Griffith, testified that while he had provided the usual 40 rounds for each of the six-pound curricle guns attached to the army, he had only been able to get off one round apiece from each of them since his men fled the field at the outset of the engagement, taking the priming horns with them!

F3: Conductor 1748

The Royal Artillery prided itself on its professionalism, but as in many other armies of the time, was forced by Treasury constraints to rely upon civilians to actually transport the guns. Although these drivers were not subject to military discipline their recruitment was far from being a haphazard process. Arrangements would be made at the outset of a campaign, or even on a fairly long term basis with conductors (haulage contractors) who provided both the horses and the personnel required and saw to it that they moved the guns in roughly the right direction. Contemporary paintings show that these drivers did not wear military uniform as such, but were easily recognised by their drab coloured waggoners' smocks and occasionally by some form of uniform headgear provided by the haulage firm for which they worked. The conductors also pleased themselves as to how they were dressed, but often opted for a semi-military style and this reconstruction is once again based on a figure in Morier's painting of the encampment at Roermond.

G1: Gunner, 4th Bn Royal Artillery 1777

Being administered by the Board of Ordnance rather than the Horse Guards, the uniforms of the Royal Artillery were not covered by the Royal Warrant of 19 December 1768. But somebody must have mentioned this to the Board because,

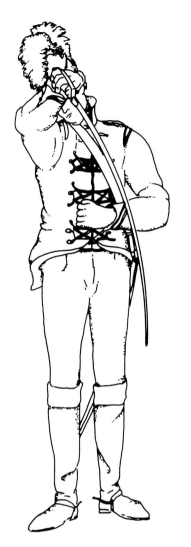

Trooper 16th Light Dragoons demonstrating the Horse near side Protect. After sketch in Rules and Regulations for the Sword Exercise in the Cavalry 1796. *Note the curious arrangement of the lace on the jacket, and the high boots. (Author)*

on 21 February 1769, they rather belatedly noted: 'His Majesty has given certain regulations for the cloathing of the several marching Regiments which may occasion some small alterations in the cloathing of the Royal Regiment of Artillery...'. Some dithering then followed until it was realised that by then it was too late to alter the clothing already ordered for that year and so new patterns were not sealed until January 1770. When they eventually appeared the new uniforms substantially followed the infantry in style and white small-clothes replaced the blue ones, except in the

invalid companies who clung to the old pattern. Still, white accoutrements were not ordered until 1772 and the coat linings were not ordered to be changed from red to white until 1782. Even then it still took over a year to get everybody into the new uniforms and even longer to replace the old embroidered drummers' caps with bearskin ones.

Cocked hats bound with yellow tape were still prescribed for gunners but one of the von Germann sketches shows a gunner serving under General Burgoyne wearing a light infantry cap. In March 1777, the Board ordered a pattern jacket, waistcoat and breeches to be made up for the gunners about to be sent to America. The waistcoat and breeches were to be the same pattern and price as those already ordered for the Artificer Company at Gibraltar, but the jacket was evidently a new pattern priced at 17s 1d apiece. As this is very close to the 17s 6d paid at the time for an ordinary soldier's coat, it may be inferred that these jackets had lapels and were not the single-breasted round jackets which became increasingly popular during this period. The gunner depicted by von Germann is presumably wearing one of these new jackets rather than a cropped coat.

The Royal Irish Artillery wore a uniform similar to their counterparts on the English establishment, but a watercolour sketch of c.1773 shows a white lining to the coat and buttons arranged in pairs, with a light dragoon-style cuff and chevrons of lace on the lower arm. Predictably a harp badge is worn on the cartouche box, but perhaps the most unusual feature shown in the watercolour is a very long Prussian-style queue reaching down into the small of the gunner's back.

G2: Officer, Corps of Engineers 1778

Engineers were also the responsibility of the Board of Ordnance, but their military status was at first somewhat ambiguous and some officers obtained their commissions by serving in infantry regiments. This was obviously a far from satisfactory state of affairs and on 14 May 1757 officers were for the first time commissioned as Engineers. Until that time, there was no prescribed uniform for engineers and many

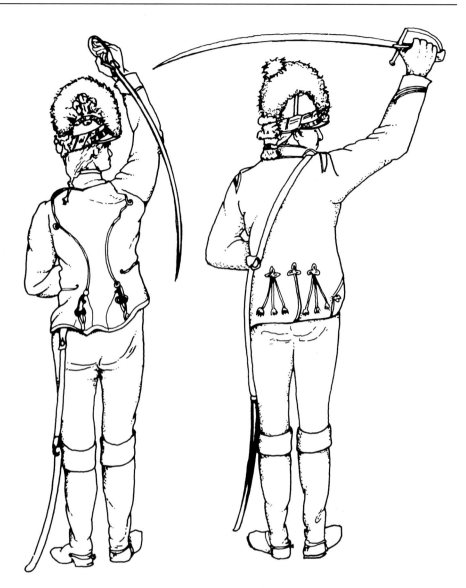

Rear view of troopers of the 10th and 16th Light Dragoons from the same source. Note the loose, comfortable fit of the jackets, especially that worn by the trooper of the 10th on the left. (Author)

apparently wore the uniform of whichever infantry regiment they then happened to belong to. This also had to change and just two weeks later the *Ipswich Journal* of all things noted that the uniform of the newly formed Corps of Engineers was 'red lapelled with black velvet, buff waistcoats and breeches'. Perhaps because there were so few of them the Board of Ordnance took rather a long time to get round to considering the modernisation of their uniforms in the wake of the 1768 Warrant and it was not until 20 August 1772 that the pattern shown in this reconstruction was authorised. As it happened, this particular uniform did not last very long. In December 1782 it was ordered to be changed to a blue coat again

faced with black velvet and lined with white.

G3: Military Artificer 1786

All Engineers were officers and prior to 1772 all the army's labouring work was carried out either by infantrymen or by civilian contractors working under engineer's direction. Every summer for many years parties of soldiers laboured on General Wade's network of roads in the Scottish Highlands. Roadwork was apparently popular as it attracted extra pay and was generally characterised by much looser discipline than usual. But it was only practical to employ soldiers as workmen during peacetime and at the same time difficult to find skilled craftsmen during wartime, especially in remote areas. Consequently in 1772, a Soldier Artificer Company was formed for service in Gibraltar. The experiment was a considerable success and led to the formation of a Corps of Royal Military Artificers and Labourers in 1787.

The Gibraltar company's uniform comprised a plain red coat faced with orange-yellow, white waistcoat and breeches. This figure is wearing the company's working dress, a fairly long red wool jacket with large side pockets – a white linen version similar to those used by the 25th on Minorca was worn in summer.

When the Corps of Royal Military Artificers and Labourers was formed an entirely new uniform was adopted, closely conforming in colour at least to that worn by Engineer officers. The full dress uniform was a dark blue coat faced black and lined white, but their working dress was similar in style to the Gibraltar company. Originally white Russia duck jackets were worn but in 1792 dark blue cloth ones were authorised for use in winter. In 1789 the Gibraltar Artificers also adopted blue coats faced black, but the two units were not combined until 1797.

H1: Officer, Royal Artillery 1794

Loutherberg's sketches of the siege of Valenciennes provide a useful illustration of how regulation and practice could often part company. Round hats actually appear to have been worn by all ranks of the Royal Artillery at this time, until the order came to replace them with the more usual cocked hats in April 1796. The order was evidently an unpopular one, because subsequently on 23 May a sternly worded reminder came instructing officers to provide themselves with the required cocked hats by the 4th of the following month.

In 1794 officers were also supposed to be wearing cloth (wool) or kerseymere breeches and top boots bound with white leather. However this unknown officer actually appears to be wearing a pair of gaiter trousers rolled up over his boots. The prescribed sword was the so-called 1786 pattern or spadroon – a straight bladed weapon. But Mercer, who had joined the Royal Artillery at this time, refers to the occasional use of a dirk instead.

H2: Gunner, 2/Madras Artillery 1790

The dress of the East India Company's artillerymen, who were invariably Europeans, broadly conformed to regular army styles. But as this reconstruction based on a watercolour by a Company artist shows, there were some significant differences. The most obvious, of course, is the hat. Instead of the ubiquitous round hat worn in the Indies by regular units of infantry and artillery from the 1770s onwards, this appears to be an early forerunner of the 19th-century solar topee. It was made of cloth stretched over a split cane frame. The blue coat turned up with red also differs from the regular army pattern in having cavalry-style chevrons of thin yellow lace on the cuff and forearm. Double-breasted waistcoats were quite popular among regular officers, but rarely worn by the rank and file. It is not clear whether they were worn by all ranks of the Madras Artillery at this time or whether this soldier has merely chosen to cut a dash by wearing one of his own while 'walking out'.

H3: Gunner, Invalid Battalion, Royal Artillery 1793

Each of the four battalions of the Royal Artillery included two invalid companies until about 1784 when they were consolidated into a single battalion under a Major Whitmore. Comprised of officers and soldiers no longer fit enough for active service in the field, their task was to man the guns in fortresses and other fixed positions. In practice, this was not always as easy as it might at first appear, since fortress guns were invariably of a large and heavy calibre. Consequently, it seems to have been the practice to employ invalid gunners to instruct and direct detachments of volunteers drawn from any infantry units which may have been handy.

On 8 March 1771, the Board of Ordnance, then still trying hard to catch up with the changes ordered to infantry uniforms in the 1768 Warrant, paused to consider the clothing of the invalid companies and had 'thoughts of making some alterations therein'. The precise nature of these alterations is not clear. But four days later the usual contractor, Mrs Elizabeth Benford, was ordered to make the coats for the invalid companies plain, 'but in all other respects the same as the present pattern'. Since Mrs Benford was also asked to report 'what abatement she will make for the lace and sewing on' it is likely that the reference to the coats being made plain means that they were unlaced.

Another thing likely to have been considered by the Board at this time was whether or not to alter the small-clothes from blue to white. In 1784 however, Major Whitmore obtained permission from the Board to have his men's breeches made with a fall-down flap as in the marching companies, which suggests that until that time they had still been wearing the old style blue breeches with a fly front. Although he succeeded in having the cut brought up to date, no alteration was made in the colour, and in a list of prices approved for the clothing of the Royal Artillery in 1792 specific mention is made of blue cloth waistcoats and breeches for invalids.

Notes sur les planches en couleurs

A Cavalerie régulière vers 1740. **A1** Soldat de cavalerie, 2nd [Royal North British] Dragoons 1748. Le manteau est à double boutonnage et gansé d'un mince galon blanc sur les boutonnières et une aiguillette sur la droite. Il porte un pantalon collant de la couleur des parements du régiment. Le filet est bleu avec un chardon et la devise NEMO ME IMPUNE LACESSIT est brodée sur le revers blanc. L'arrière du calot est rouge sur fond bleu et le calot est gansé de jaune. **A2** est un Officer des 2nd [Montagu's] Dragoon Guards vers 1747. Parmi les accoutrements, citons une grande ceinture pour l'épée et une boîte à cartouche à bandoulière sur l'épaule gauche. **A3** est un Farrier 11th [Kerr's] Dragoons, 1748. Il porte un calot de fourrure et un manteau bleu aux revers de la couleur des parements du régiment. Sa pèlerine est une pèlerine ordinaire de soldat de cavalerie, et la doublure est de la couleur des parements du régiment.

B Jacobite Emergency 1745/6. **B1** Soldat de cavalerie, Duke of Cumberland's Hussars. L'uniforme vert et cramoisi et la livrée personnelle du duc. Il porte des bottes de style dragon, la verte non gansée remplace le dolman et une pelisse assez longue. **B2** est un Private Gentleman, Yorkshire Hunters, habillés de bleu gansé de rouge avec des boutons dorés, calot gansé d'or, bottes et selles légères. **B3** est un simple soldat, Georgia Rangers. Les sources contemporaines mentionnent seulement un uniforme vert et un calot en cuir.

C Guerre de Sept Ans. **C2** Sergent, Light Troop 2nd Dragoons, 1756. Il porte des bottes de jockey légères avec bande ridige et un calot en cuir. La visière du calot est remontée et porte le chiffre royal et le numéro du régiment, ainsi qu'une couronne en cuivre sur le crâne. A part le numéro, la seule distinction autorisée pour les régiments était une touffe de crin, une moitié rouge et l'autre moitié de la couleur des parements du régiment. **C2** est un officier des 13th [Douglas's] Dragoons, 1767. Les boutons et les boucles en galon doré sont par groupes de trois et ils portent un pantalon collant blanc. **C3** Soldat de cavalerie 21st Light Dragoons [Royal Foresters], 1760. Le casque et de style allemand. Son manteau est à revers et l'équipement du cheval comprend un grand shabraque de style hussard en chèvre blanche. Tous les rangs ont un badge bleu sur la fonte de selle, qui porte le numéro du régiment et le chiffre royal en blanc ou argent.

D La Guerre américaine. **D1** Simple soldat Infanterie Légère, Light Dragoons. Ils recevaient une pèlerine ou cape au lieu du manteau, qu'ils portaient par dessus leur paquetage. Ils avaient des guêtres en tissu marron et un casque en cuir. Chaque homme portait une hachette. **D2** Sergent, 17th Light Dragoons 1776. **D3** Soldat de cavalerie, Castleknock Horse 1779. L'uniforme, en particulier le casque, est de style très français et il convient de noter le sabre de forme curieuse mais pourtant relativement commune à l'époque.

E1 Officier, 7th Dragoons 1770. Cet officier, basé sur un portrait, porte un manteau à boutonnage simple, passé de mode à cette date. Les 7èmes étaient censés avoir des parements blancs mais sur le portrait un ton de beige très distinctif est utilisé pour les parements et le pantalon collant. **E2**, soldat de cavalerie, 16th Light Dragoons 1790. La veste est bleu foncé et de style dolman hussard, gansée de blanc. Une seconde veste sans manches était portée par dessus, sans doute pour se protéger du froid. **E3** Le capitaine Alexander Grant, Garde du corps du Gouverneur de Madras. L'infanterie légère portait une veste légère verte aux parements rouge et un calot, une culotte et des bas avec des guêtres noires.

F Royal Artillery. **F1** Forbes MacBean, 1748, porte l'uniforme traditionnel des canonniers : manteau bleu foncé aux parements rouges mais distingué des soldats du rang par son gilet et sa culotte rouges. **F2** Canonnier, Royal Artillery 1748. Ses guêtres sont noires, comme normale durant une campagne et, à la différence de ces officiers, cet homme porte un pantalon collant bleu. A la taille, sur une ceinture mince, il porte une boîte de forme assez curieuse ainsi qu'un porte-baionnette noir. **F3** Chauffeur 1788. Ces conducteurs ne portaient pas un uniforme militaire à proprement parler mais on les reconnaissait facilement grâce à leur tablier marron de voituriers et de temps à autre par un couvre-chef uniforme fourni par la société de transport pour laquelle ils travaillaient. Ils choisissaient leurs vêtements mais préféraient souvent un style semi-militaire.

Farbtafeln

A Reguläre Kavallerie um 1740. **A1** Soldat, 2nd [Royal North British] Dragoons, 1748. Der Waffenrock ist zweireihig, tressenlos mit schmalen, weißen Litzenbändern an den Knopflöchern und einer Bandschleife auf der rechten Schulter. Der Soldat trägt Kniehosen in der Besatzfarbe des Regiments. Das Mützenband ist blau und zeigt eine Distel. Auf dem weißen Aufschlag steht NEMO ME IMPUNE LACESSIT. Die Rückseite der Mütze ist rot über blau, und das ganze ist gelb gepaspelt. **A** Diese Abbildung zeigt einen Offizier der 2nd [Montagu's] Dragoon Guards, ca. 1747. Zur Ausrüstung gehört ein stabiler Leibriemen für das Schwert sowie eine Patronentasche und ein Tragriemen über der linken Schulter. **A3** zeigt einen Farrier der 11th [Kerr's] Dragoons, 1748. Er trägt eine Pelzmütze und einen blauen Waffenrock mit Aufschlägen in der Besatzfarbe des Regiments. Sein Umhang entspricht dem roten Umhang der einfachen Soldaten und ist in der Besatzfarbe des Regiments eingefaßt.

B Der Jakobiten-Notstand, 1745/46. **B1** Soldat der Duke of Cumberland's Hussars. Bei der grün-purpurroten Uniform handelt es sich um die persönliche Livree des Herzogs. Die Abbildung zeigt Stiefel im Dragonerstil, die tressenlose Jacke, die anstatt eines Dolman getragen wird, und einen recht langen Übermantel. **B2** Private Gentleman bei den Yorkshire Hunters. Diese hatten blaue Kleidung mit scharlachroten Besätzen und Goldknöpfen, Mützen mit Goldlitzen, helle Stiefel und Sättel. **B3** Gefreiter der Georgia Rangers. Berichte aus der damaligen Zeit verweisen lediglich auf eine grüne Uniform und eine Ledermütze.

C Der Siebenjährige Krieg. **C1** Feldwebel, Light Troop 2nd Dragoons, 1756. Er trägt leichte Jockeystiefel mit steifem Schaft und eine Ledermütze. Die Mütze weist einen aufgeschlagenen Frontstreifen auf, auf dem das königliche Monogramm und die Regimentsnummer erscheint. Auf dem Mützendeckel ist eine Messingkur. Abgesehen von der Nummer war als einziges Regimentsabzeichen eine Quaste aus Roßhaar zugelassen, die halb rot und halb in der Waffenfarbe der Einheit war. **C2** Offizier der 13th [Douglas's] Dragoons, 1767. Die Knöpfe und die goldfarbenen Tressenschlaufen sind in Dreierreihen angeordnet, und man trägt weiße Kniehosen. **C3** Soldat der 21st Light Dragoons [Royal Foresters], 1760. Der Helm entspricht dem deutschen Stil. Der Waffenrock hat Revers, und zur Pferdeausrüstung gehört eine große Schabracke im Husarenstil aus weißem Ziegenleder. Alle Ränge hatten ein blaues Abzeichen auf der Pistolentasche, das die Regimentsnummer aufwies sowie das königliche Monogramm in weiß beziehungsweise silber.

D Der Amerikanische Unabhängigkeitskrieg. **D1** Gefreiter, Light Infantry Troop, 16th Light Dragoons. Diese Soldaten erhielten einen weiten Umhang oder einen Mantel anstatt des Umhangs, den sie über ihrem Rucksack trugen. Sie hatten braune Stoffgamaschen und einen Lederhelm. **D2**: Feldwebel, 17th Light Dragoons, 1776. **D3** Soldat, Castleknock Horse, 1779. Die Uniform und insbesondere der Helm sind dem Stil nach sehr französisch. Bemerkenswert ist auch der Säbel in recht merkwürdiger Form, obwohl er zu dieser Zeit keineswegs ungewöhnlich war.

E1 Offizier, 7th Dragoons, 1770. Die Abbildung dieses Offiziers, die auf einem Porträt beruht, zeigt den zu dieser Zeit eher altmodischen, einreihigen Waffenrock. Eigentlich sollen die 7th Dragoons weiße Besätze gehabt haben, doch zeigt das Porträt eindeutig einen gelbbraunen Farbton bei den Besätzen und den Kniehosen. **E2** Einfacher Soldat der 16th Light Dragoons, 1790. Die Jacke ist ein dunkelblauer Dolman im Husarenstil mit weißem Tressenbesatz. **E3** Captain Alexander Grant, Leibwächter des Gouverneurs von Madras. Die leichte Infanterie trug eine leichte grüne Jacke mit roten Besätzen, eine Mütze, Breeches mit angenähten Strümpfen und schwarze Gamaschen.

F: Royal Artillery. **F1** Forbes MacBean, 1748, trägt die traditionelle Kanonier-Uniform, die aus einem dunkelblauen Waffenrock mit roten Aufschlägen besteht, unterscheidet sich von den Mannschaftsgraden jedoch durch seine rote Weste und Breeches. **F2** Kanonier, Royal Artillery, 1748. Die Gamaschen sind schwarz, wie das bei Feldzügen gang und gäbe war, und im Gegensatz zu seinen Offizieren trägt dieser Soldat blaue Kniehosen. An einem schmalen Gürtel um die Taille

G1 Canonnier, 4th Batallion Royal Artillery 1777. Il porte un calot d'infanterie légère et un manteau bleu foncé avec des boutons de cuivre. G2 Officier, Corps of Engineers 1778. L'uniforme du Corps of Engineers nouvellement formé avait des revers rouges avec du velours noir, un gilet et une culotte grèges. G3 Artificier militaire 1786. Ce personnage prote l'uniforme de travail de sa compagnie, une veste de laine rouge assez longue avec de grandes poches. En été, elle était remplacée par une version en lin blanc.

H1 Officier de la Royal Artillery 1794. Les officiers étaient également censés porter une culotte de tissu [laine] ou de kerseymere et des bottes attachées par des liens en cuir blanc. Celui-ci semble porter une culotte roulée par dessus ses bottes. H2 Canonnier, 2/Madras Artillery 1790. Le chapeau est en tissu étiré par dessus une armature en osier fendu. Le manteau bleu aux revers rouges a des chevrons de style cavalerie sur les revers et l'avant-bras. Les officers réguliers aimaient porter un gilet à double boutonnage, peu adopté par les rangs. H3, Canonnier, Invalid Battalion, Royal Artillery 1793. Le manteau des compagnies d'invalides était d'une seule couleur mais à part cela était le même que celui des autres unités, porté avec un gilet et une culotte de toile bleue.

sieht man eine Bauchtasche von recht merkwürdiger Form und eine schwarze Bajonett-Schlaufe. F3 Transporteur, 1748. Diese Fahrer trugen an sich keine Militäruniform, waren an ihren mattbraunen Fuhrmannskitteln jedoch leicht zu erkennen. Manchmal hatten sie auch eine Art gleichförmiger Kopfbedeckung auf, die ihre Transportfirma zur Verfügung stellte. Welche Kleidung sie trugen, blieb ihnen überlassen, doch entschieden sie sich häufig für einen halb-militärischen Stil.

G1 Kanonier, 4th Bn Royal Artillery, 1777. Er trägt eine leichte Infanteriemütze und einen dunkelblauen Rock mit Messingknöpfen. G2 Offizier, Corps of Engineers, 1778. Die Uniform dieses neu aufgestellten Korps war rot mit schwarzen Samtrevers, gelbbraunen Westen und Breeches. G Military Artificer, 1786. Diese Figur trägt die Arbeitskleidung der Kompanie, eine ziemlich lange, rote Wolljacke mit großen Seitentaschen - im Sommer trug man eine Jacke aus weißem Leinen.

H1 Offizier der Royal Artillery, 1794. Eigentlich sollten auch Offiziere Breeches aus Wollstoff ("Kerseymere") tragen sowie Überstiefel, die mit weißem Leder gebunden waren. Dieser Offizier scheint jedoch ein paar Gamaschenhosen zu tragen, die über seine Stiefel gerollt sind. H2 Kanonier, 2/Madras Artillery, 1790. Der Hut ist aus Stoff, der über ein Rohrgestell gezogen wurde. Der blaue Rock mit roten Aufschlägen weist kavallerieähnliche Winkel aus schmaler, gelber Litze an den Manschetten und auf dem Vorderarm auf. Bei den meisten regulären Offizieren waren zweireihige Westen sehr beliebt, die jedoch von den Mannschaftsgraden selten getragen wurden. H3 Kanonier, Invalid Battalion, Royal Artillery, 1793. Die Waffenröcke dieser Kompanien waren tressenlos, glichen jedoch ansonsten denen der anderen Einheiten. Sie wurden mit blauen Stoffwesten und Breeches getragen.